This Little Piggy Got Divorced
Written by Amy Poon
Illustrations Eun-Kyung Kang
Publisher Spy Publishing
Design Studio McLoughlin
Printers Empress Litho Ltd.
PR Kirsten Orchard

Telephone +44 (0)20 8987 6970
Email info@spypublishing.com
Website www.thislittlepiggywenttoprada.com

First published in the United Kingdom by
Spy Publishing Ltd
2nd Floor, 334 Chiswick High Road
London W4 5TA
United Kingdom

British Library Cataloguing-in-Publication Data
A catalogue record of this book is available from the British Library.
ISBN 978-0-9544964-8-7

THIS LITTLE PIGGY
GOT DIVORCED

Acknowledgements

To all the boys and girls who did it, survived it, shared it with me and tried to show me the right way – you know who you are.
Dr Pam for restoring my sanity and giving me the courage.
FH for trying to do the right thing and not heeding all the advice of "The Barracuda".
Mr. & Mrs. Tin for a writer's haven at Château Orchard and being the ultimate hosts, in absentia.
Aunty Pet, a barrister of swan-like grace, fearsome intellect and immense kindness.
Percy Pig for listening and listening again and reading and rereading, and awesomeness and attractiveness for which there was no charge.
Chris Collier, the MOST patient, understanding and long-suffering of agents.
Ali for crossing i's and dotting t's and pulling me through the second-book syndrome.
Mr & Mrs Smith for making it possible all over again...
Martin M for being ridiculously clever and wonderful and for believing in Piggy in all her guises.
Zebby for more creatively spilt coffee and imagination.
David M for putting ink to paper.
Kirsten Orchard for her invaluable media advice and support.
Thanks also to the team at Spy: Aline Keuroghlian, Laura Mizon, Jasmine Darby and Anthony Leyton.
And finally, Beethoven for backing a "Mon Mome".

For Mimi

Because you're probably going to go into therapy anyway so I might as well give you a real reason...

divorce /*di-vōrs'*, *-vörs* / the legal dis-
solution of a marriage or the decree that
dissolves it; complete separation or sev-
erance *(fig)*. [Fr, from L *dīvortium*, from
dīvortere, another form of *dīvertere* (of a
woman) to leave one's husband]

There was a young woman who lived in her Choos,
Though she once had a house in a smart Chelsea Mews.
SO MUCH on Jimmy,
The house had to go,
And with it, the Amex and husband in tow!

The Benefit of Hindsight

Once upon a time, a beautiful, accomplished, *intelligent* young woman was walking through the woods where she chanced upon a frog.

The frog boldly stopped the young woman in her tracks and said, "Beautiful lady, I was once a handsome prince but a wicked witch cast a spell on me and turned me into a frog. The spell can only be broken by a kiss. If you *kiss* me, I will turn back into a handsome prince and I will marry you so you can come to live in my castle and be my queen, bear my children, care for me, look after my affairs, my family, and my social life and *we will live happily ever after.*"

That evening, as the beautiful, accomplished, intelligent young woman dined in the company of her beautiful, accomplished, intelligent friends, on a dish of delicately sautéed frogs' legs, she thought to herself,

"I don't think so!"

Early on in my marriage, secure in the blind faith that we were to be married till death did us part, I used to refer to my now ex-husband as my "first husband". It was a term of endearment, albeit a perverse one, but it was meant with love and humour. Then, one day my first husband said to me,

I marvelled at his wit and humour and thought, "What a very clever man I have married!"

Marriage Vs. Divorce

Engaged: 1 year

Married: 5 years

Cost of Wedding: £36.863

Cost of Marriage counselling: £22.800

Value of Wedding present: £35.261

Value of divorce settlement: £216.000

It would seem that getting divorced is significantly more expensive than getting married, yet roughly one in two of us do it – which says an awful lot…

The Big P

lack Dream

I am told that most girls growing up have a perfect white dream – a vision of their ideal wedding day with yards of white lace and silk, an abundance of orange blossom, rivers of champagne and, of course, Prince Charming standing tall and proud, positively glowing with love and adoration, at the altar.

I never had the big white dream. Instead,
I harboured with relish and guilty
pleasure my big black dream: I walked
down the aisle adorned with blood red
roses and celosia the texture of velvet.
in a perfectly tailored black Roland
Mouret Galaxy dress, a perfectly trained
miniature dachshund called Ulysses at my
Louboutin heels, behind the coffin of my
dead husband.

I don't deny this is macabre for a child.
but in the immediate aftermath of
divorce, or more likely in the process,
this might be a more common dream that
we'd like to admit…

17

The Official Process

To get divorced in Britain you must have been married for more than one year. (You see, even the law doesn't give you much of a fighting chance!) You must complete a form, called a 'Petition', giving the reasons why you are applying, to show your marriage is definitely over. If you have children you also complete a form called the 'Statement of Arrangements' in which you tell the court what plans you have made for the children once the divorce is final.

Perhaps the most important thing you'll write on your divorce petition is the reason why your marriage has come to an end. In the eyes of the law, you have to prove "irretrievable breakdown of the marriage" and currently there are five main ways to explain what has lead to the breakdown.

Adultery: You don't actually have to name the "third party" with whom the adultery was committed. but you do have to prove to the satisfaction of the court that the adultery has taken place. Unfortunately, if you embarked on an affair in an effort to end your marriage, you cannot cite your own adultery – it doesn't count!

A sympathetic (male) lawyer I know said to his client on the justification of her affair, "Well. if your husband has behaved in such a way as to drive you into the arms of another man. I would say he has been behaving very unreasonably."

Choosing the right lawyer is VERY important!

Unreasonable behaviour: If you think that your spouse has behaved so unreasonably that you cannot possibly be expected to live with him. you have a case for divorce.

Your reasons will be very subjective. but whether it's treating the marital home like a hotel. refusing to take out the rubbish. or using bad language. any competent lawyer will be able to fashion a convincing case under the unreasonable behaviour banner. This is the part where you can let rip and call your spouse every name under the sun and your hopefully lovely lawyer will translate your no doubt justified venom into perfectly respectable legalese.

Two years separation with consent:
This is undoubtedly the most civilised
way to go, if you can wait that long.
You both have to agree that the
marriage has broken down, but no
reasons are necessary. The snag is the
time period. You can, however, back-
date your separation, claiming that
you have already been separated for
two years when you file, as long as any
children you have are over the age of
fifteen months.

The legal definition of separation here
is interesting. You can actually still
live under the same roof but you must
satisfy the court that you are living
separate lives: that is, you don't cook,
clean, eat or interact together. If this
is the definition of a legal separation,
then a vast number of marrieds I know
are technically separated.

Desertion for two years: If your
spouse has left you for a period of two
years or more, that will be sufficient
for the court to grant a decree. If your
husband has left you for a period of
two years, you should be celebrating
and moving on!

Desertion for five years: A respondent
to a petition on this ground could not
resist a decree being granted, even on
religious grounds.

So, failing all else, either make your
husband disappear for five years or...

disappear
yourself

On the morning of my standard court hearing, my kindly, sympathetic lawyer met me in front of the grand and imposing façade of the Family Law Courts.

"Good news!" he said. "We have a nice judge – very practical, no-nonsense, modern woman. Not at all like the chap I had last week."

"What happened last week?" I asked.

"Well, I had a client – similar to yourself, separated for two years but living under the same roof. The judge was an older avuncular figure, part of the establishment for decades. He was rather doubtful of the separation arrangements and said

"Mr. Coe, your client is an extremely attractive young woman. I find it very hard to believe that her husband has managed to live under the same roof as her for two years and not have had sex with her."

The entire court room, as you can imagine, was reduced to hysterics."

I pondered this for a while and replied, "I wish you hadn't told me this, because if the judge doesn't say that about me, I shall be extremely upset!"

Form D8

It is somewhat sobering and anticlimactic seeing your entire married life set down in writing on a tidy little form of usually not more than five pages. It reads like a rather dull fact sheet: name, date of birth, where you were married, address etc. etc. etc. Most of it seems unnecessarily formal but how else can divorce lawyers justify their £450+VAT/hour fees?

If you are divorcing on the grounds of separation or desertion then the form is relatively straightforward. If however you are divorcing on the grounds of adultery or unreasonable behaviour then things become more complicated.

Section 13 is where divorce lawyers really do deserve their hard-earned pennies, detailing the particulars of your irretrievably broken down marriage with what you will no doubt consider to be superlative understatement.

"Unreasonable Behaviour"

(13) Particulars

The said marriage has broken down irretrievably by reason of the Respondent's unreasonable behaviour.

PARTICULARS

What you told your lawyer and your best friend: *"My husband is a moody, ungrateful, selfish, unfeeling bastard"*

How your lawyer might translate this: *The Respondent has a sullen and moody disposition and does not appreciate all that the Petitioner does on his behalf. The Petitioner has made every effort to accommodate the Respondent and his demands and he has continually failed to show the Petitioner any*

form of gratitude.

What you told your lawyer and your best friend: *"My husband has turned into a raving alcoholic. Last night he came home from work and had six beers, two bottles of wine and half a bottle of cognac, then kicked in the bathroom door before passing out in the corridor."*

How your lawyer might translate this: *The Respondent has started to use alcohol more frequently, with the result that his behaviour is erratic and he suffers from violent mood swings.*

Other examples of "unreasonable behavior" that have been cited in section 13 of various divorce petitions:

a. The Petitioner has supported the Respondent in his business, and has been demeaned for her efforts.

b. The Respondent has a bullying and patronising manner and frequently insults the Petitioner's attempts to be useful. He makes pejorative remarks about the Petitioner and her abilities in front of others, including in front of friends, family and work colleagues. This has left the Petitioner feeling depressed and with low self-esteem.

c. On XXX date, the Respondent shouted at the Petitioner while the parties' son was present. The Respondent called the Petitioner a 'bitch' repeatedly. The parties' son was extremely frightened and distressed by this.

d. The Respondent has subjected the Petitioner to both physical and verbal abuse, and on XXX date he pushed her so she fell to the ground, causing bruising to her head and face.

e. On XXX date, the Respondent had consumed alcohol to excess. This led to him intimidating the Petitioner at a dinner party by behaving in an aggressive manner. The Petitioner had to leave the dinner party because she was so frightened by the Respondent.

f. On XXX date, shortly after the dinner party referred to above, the Petitioner left the matrimonial home as she was concerned about her and her son's safety and about the unpredictable behaviour of the Respondent which has been a source of great stress and unhappiness to her.

g. When the Petitioner was away from the matrimonial home, the Respondent destroyed one of the Petitioner's paintings and set fire to the Petitioner's car.

h. The Respondent's attempts to curb his irrational behaviour have not been successful.

Adultery

I have always wondered why adultery should be in a category of its own as a reason for divorce. Does it make it more or less acceptable than unreasonable behaviour? Contrary to what you would expect, adultery petitions are pretty boring. They read something like: "The Respondent has, to the Petitioner's knowledge, committed within the past x months several acts of adultery with a person who is known to the Petitioner, but who is not named in this petition."

The adultery has either to be proved against the Respondent or admitted by the Respondent. As adultery is surprisingly hard (and expensive) to prove if your spouse is unwilling to admit it, it will usually be included in the "unreasonable behaviour" particulars.

I think it rather touching that a divorce petition ends with a "prayer" that the marriage be dissolved and that the Petitioner be granted relief. It's enough really to turn the most hardened atheist into a hair shirt-wearing, self-flagellating born-again believer.

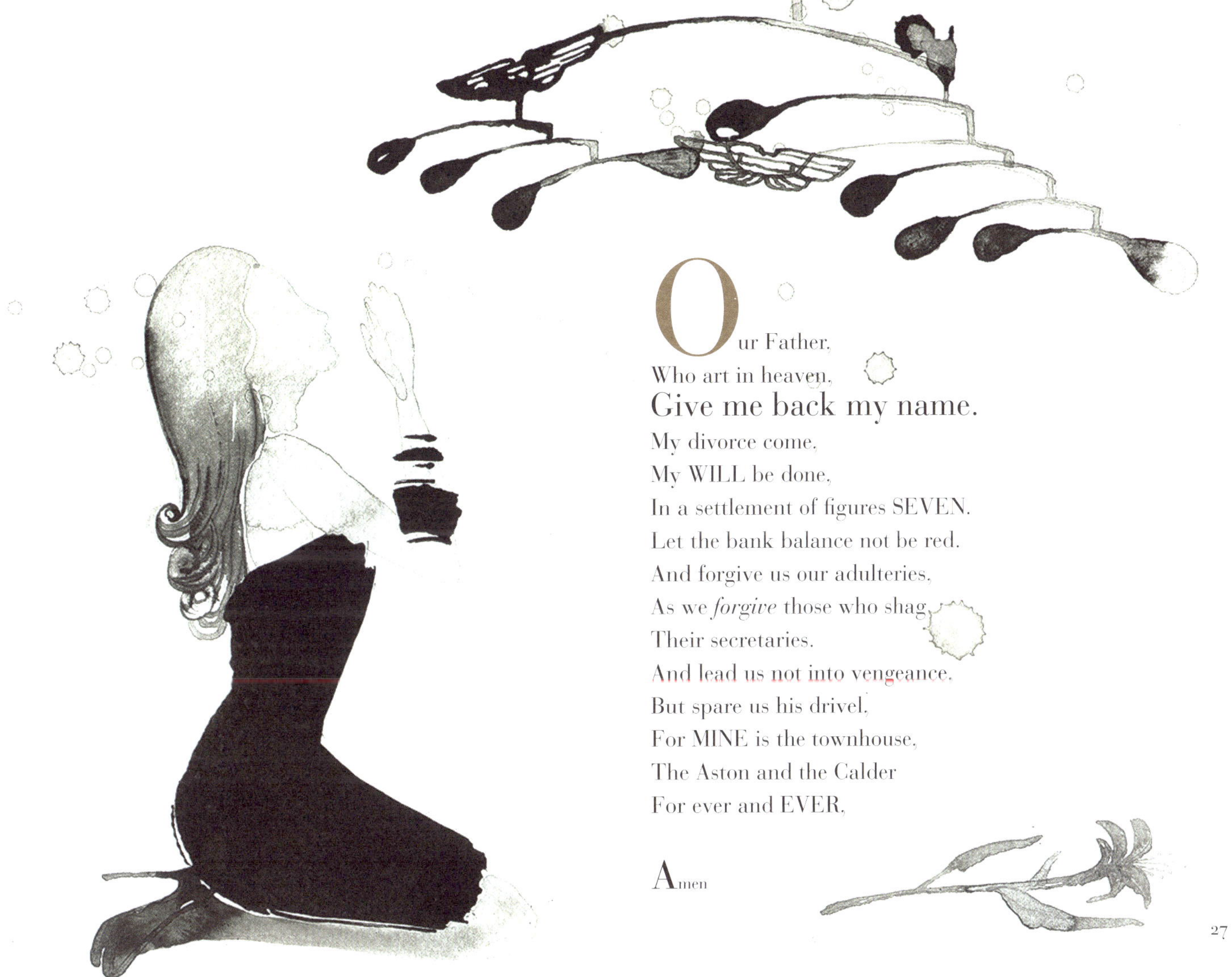
Our Father,
Who art in heaven,
Give me back my name.
My divorce come,
My WILL be done,
In a settlement of figures SEVEN.
Let the bank balance not be red.
And forgive us our adulteries,
As we forgive those who shag
Their secretaries.
And lead us not into vengeance.
But spare us his drivel,
For MINE is the townhouse,
The Aston and the Calder
For ever and EVER,

Amen

The Emotional Process

The

Once you navigate your way around the inappropriately formal jargon, the legal process is quite clear and simple. What is not quite so clear and simple is the emotional process, which is as easy to understand as *Finnegan's Wake* translated into Swahili and written in the sand.

There is a terrible place before you decide to divorce. It's called Limbo. In Limbo, you are daily torn between "making it work" and walking out immediately. You can be here for months or years, but a very wise woman once said to me, "Let the chips fall where they may," meaning in Limbo, you can't really deal with anything real. You're waiting and seeing.

What got me out of Limbo was when my therapist told me something that made more sense to me than sixteen months of marriage counselling: It is very important that you leave a man before you start to hate him, particularly if the man in question happens to be the father of your child.

They say divorce follows the same emotional cycle as death: shock, anger, grief, acceptance. These phases are not mutually exclusive. In many cases, with shock, there may also be relief, which doesn't mean you won't also feel anger and sadness. They also say women mourn their marriages before they leave them and men after their wives have left them – probably because they are left so suddenly to fend for themselves. People used to say they felt a sense of failure when finally leaving a marriage. More commonly nowadays, people cite a sense of relief, joy and freedom.

He loves me
I Love him not
I Love him
He loves me
Not
I Love him

Y ou may never be able to distil the exact reasons for wanting to get divorced but you know things are not what they should be when you:

1. Have sex with your spouse solely to fulfil your conjugal duty then count the numbers of days with dread until you have to do it again. 2. Look among your friends and acquaintances for your replacement. 3. Slip condoms into your husband's washbag when he goes away on business trips. 4. Have a serious affair. 5. Fall seriously in love with someone else. 6. Save up a run-away fund. 7. Engineer situations whereby your spouse might commit an indiscretion – e.g. leave him drunk and horny in the company of another drunk and horny person. 8. Are physically abused. 9. Are not able to remember the last time you had an interesting or meaningful conversation with each other – or any conversation at all for that matter. 10. Fantasise about your spouse dying in some horrible accident. 11. Deliberately, and with pleasure, do things which you know they find irritating. 12. Find all their qualities/mannerisms which you once thought endearing intensely irritating. 13. Just wish they would disappear. 14. Plan dinner parties and holidays and forget to include them. 15. Plan endless social engagements so you never have to be with your spouse alone.

The way you feel about your spouse during the divorce process usually continues post-divorce. Be this as it may, it is imperative for your own dignity that you speak only in the most glowing terms about your ex-spouse to everyone but your closest and most trusted friends. People always want to believe the worst, so the more glowing, your references to your ex-spouse are, the more of a rascal they will suspect him of being.

They will also ask you banal questions such as,

"What went wrong?"

Well, if you knew, you wouldn't have spent twenty-seven months' worth of mortgage repayments on trying to figure it out, would you?

Stupid questions like that deserve equally disingenuous answers such as, "He's quite brilliant, maybe just too brilliant for me."

Answers like this
a. make you sound gracious to a fault.
b. bring on a flood of denials and assurances that you are as brilliant if not more so than your ex.
c. ring so untrue as to make you sound truly long-suffering.

No-one, however incredulous, could accuse you of being vicious, underhand, petty or rallying friends to your side.

Although becoming friends with an ex-spouse is an improbable scenario, it does no harm and much good to be eventually on civil grounds with each other. This is unlikely to happen if he perceives you to have ripped off his genitals through his wallet or knows you have slept with his brother/best friend/father.

MARRIAGE

Counselling, I am told, has saved many marriages. It didn't save mine but that wasn't the counsellor's fault. My ex-husband used to always say that the only way to make someone do something is if they really want to do it.

In hindsight, perhaps you didn't really want to save your marriage but didn't have the clarity or the courage to say so at the time. Possibly you felt the pressure of at least having to try so you spent eighteen months in counselling, pretending. You didn't know at the time that you were pretending. Often you don't know – you can't – but it helps if you do know why you're going for help before you embark on a huge time commitment that is

emotionally and financially exhausting.

There must be as many kinds of marriage counsellor as there are lawyers, and many more besides.

There are the mothering types with comfy, brightly coloured armchairs in their consulting rooms. Pictures done by their children adorn the walls and holiday snapshots of their hubbies sit on their desks. They are caring, concerned, kindly – always ready with a cup of tea and a shoulder to cry on. If sympathy is all you wanted, you've come to the right place.

There are the new-age types, all flowing Indian skirts and bangles proferring chamomile tea and telling you your aura is very angry today. They urge you to seek the higher truth, to rise above your earthly worries and constraints, to find inner peace and learn tolerance, acceptance, kindness. They tell you to look into each others' souls and connect, send messages of love and forgiveness.

Then there are the Freudians, the Jungians, the X-ists and the Y-ists, asking if you might be in love with your father, if your husband was perhaps regressing to an unresolved childhood trauma, whether you were scarred by abandonment or the death of your family pet.

Counselling

Finally, if you are lucky, you come across the real thing – a truly competent, capable, knowledgeable, objective mentor who promises no miracles, who doesn't judge, criticise or condone and who patiently helps you unravel the mess you have found yourselves in. Good counsellors don't save your marriage, they save you from yourself so that you can move forward with some clarity, whatever decision you finally make.

A friend of mine spent two years in counselling before deciding to leave his marriage. In his penultimate consultation, his counsellor asked what he thought he had gained from their sessions. He duly went away and thought about it. Coming back for his last appointment, he told his counsellor he thought he had a better understanding of himself, his triggers, his situation, his wife.

The counsellor then said...

"Do you know what I think? I think you came to counselling wanting to end your marriage and you are now leaving counselling having ended your marriage."

The counsellor was absolutely right.

"It may be wrong to marry for money bu

is very foolish to divorce without it. "

Amy Poon

How well you think of your lawyer may depend on how well you are living after your Decree Absolute has been granted. The law, so precise on the legal formalities of divorce, is rather vague on the division of assets – which is the one area uppermost in people's minds when contemplating running away from their spouses.

Most of us start with the intention of being adult, fair, courteous and civilised, refusing to sink to the depths of arguing over the ownership of the master-bathroom loo brush, but in the throes of emotional turmoil, unable to bite back the ill-timed angry word, you may fight to the death for the last coffee spoon.

Generally speaking, women who have been married for any length of time are awarded half the matrimonial assets. To anyone who has half a brain, that means half of what can be gotten away with. A girlfriend once told me,

"Darling, there's his kitty, your kitty, the joint kitty and there is ALWAYS a kitty you don't know about."

Lots of things come into play when negotiating financial settlements. Because you cannot put a price on the broken dreams, the disappointment, the hurt, the anger and the pain, often it unfortunately does become a fight over the coffee machine and the Egyptian cotton towels.

The greatest hindrance to asking for what you need or want is undoubtedly guilt. Guilt at walking out, at having had an affair, at not sticking it out, at not standing by your vows. Guilt makes you do very funny things – ask

any Catholic – and guilt in financial
negotiations is fatal! You will understand
this only when, years after your decree
absolute is granted, you are living in a
rented two-up-two-down in Hounslow
while your ex-husband is comfortably
accommodated in your 7,000 sq. ft former
marital home. However much you may
feel responsible, just remember this:

"It takes two to destroy a marriage."

Margaret Trudeau, wife of Pierre Trudeau, the 15th Prime Minister of Canada

I read somewhere in my impressionable youth that "Love is an illusion, created by lawyer types to perpetuate another illusion called marriage to create a reality called divorce and thus an illusionary need for lawyers."

My cynicism in no way diminishes the opinion I have of the good work that the ladies and gentlemen of the law do on our behalf, but it is not for nothing that divorce lawyers earn nicknames like "The Barracuda."

“ I'm a very good housekeeper – every time I leave a man, I keep his house”

Zsa Zsa Gabor

Ways to get by if you didn't "do an Abramovich"[*]

The Divorce Registry

Once you have been through the house with "His" and "Hers" Post-It notes and you have finally divided and conquered – or been conquered, you often find you are missing the most banal and have acquired the most extraordinary things. This is no time for reticence or modesty. Under the circumstances, it is totally acceptable to alert your friends to your financial misfortune, particularly those who came to your wedding and did not buy you a wedding gift. Avail yourself of their guilt, generosity, love and support – in whichever way you desire them to manifest it. You can always eBay the extraordinary items.

* According to media reports, Irina Abramovich's divorce settlement is guesstimated at £1.5 billion.

Darlings,

Enough with the tea and sympathy.

As you know, my first husband and I are getting divorced.

Harry shown absolutely no interest in our Christofle silver (or any cutlery - caveman that he is) during our marriage.

He has suddenly become tenaciously attached to the soup spoons... He takes them to the office and sleeps with them under his pillow.

In the rather dull and dreary fashion of divorces, post division of assets, I am missing a fair number of essential household items.

Should you wish to celebrate my divorce with me by purchasing a gift, a list is being held with...

The Divorce Registry.

with love and thanks in anticipation

Amy X

P.S. I seem to recall that you never bought us a wedding present...

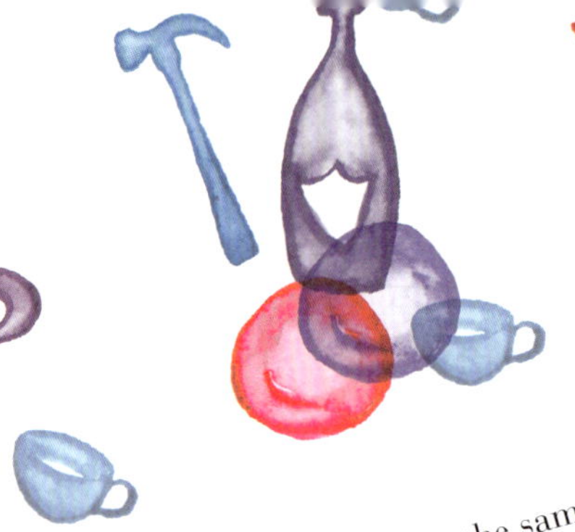

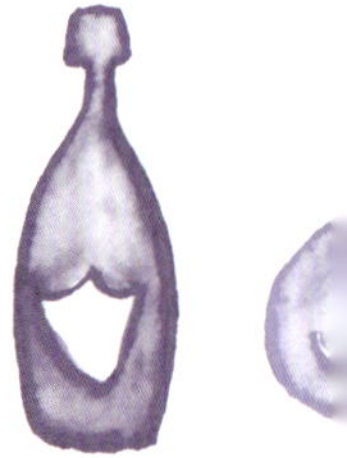

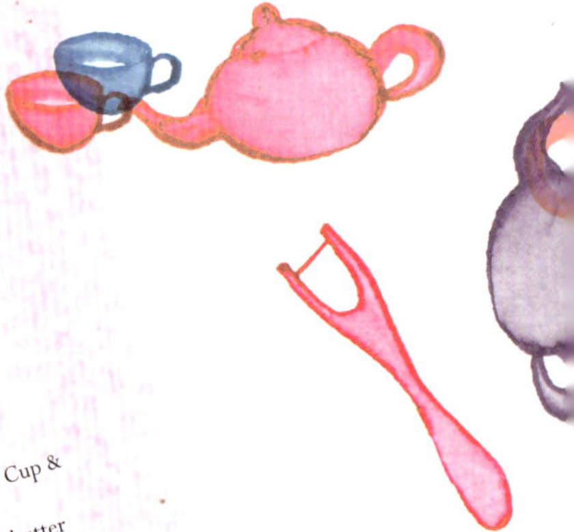

In short, your divorce list probably looks much the same as your wedding list did.

The Divorce Registry

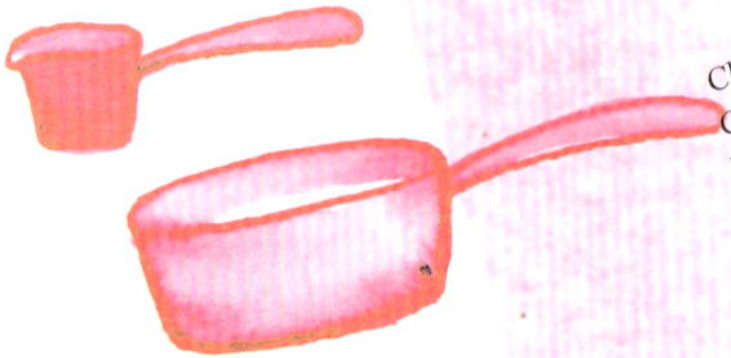

Client: Amy Poon, formerly Allen
Client No: 7396
Date of Divorce: 28th April 2009

Kitchen
6 x Walton Tea Towels – beige / cream
1 x Le Creuset Frying Pan, Granite, 26cm
1 x Le Creuset Round Casserole, Granite, 28cm
1 x Global GS Series 18cm Santoku Knife
1 x Global G Series 21cm Carving Knife
1 x Global GSF Series 8cm Peeling Knife
1 x Bredemeijer Teapot – white
1 x Portmeirion Sophie Conran, White, Covered Vegetable Dish, 27cm
Laguiole Brights Teapoons, Set of 6
che Kettle, TW911P2
Espresso Coffee

Dining
8 x Villeroy & Boch Anmut Breakfast Cup & saucer
8 x Villeroy & Boch Anmut Bread & butter plate, 16cm
8 x Villeroy & Boch Anmut Flat plate, 27cm
8 x Villeroy & Boch Anmut Deep plate, 24cm

Miscellaneous
Tool Box – complete with screwdrivers, hammer and pliers
Stuff relating to car care
Ladder
Ironing Board – if you must

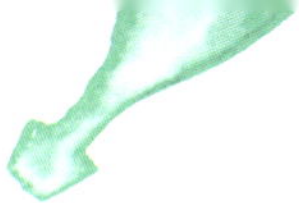

If you are in possession of your daily household necessities and you didn't leave your husband following a torrid affair, your divorce list should read something like this:

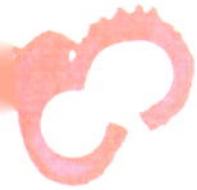

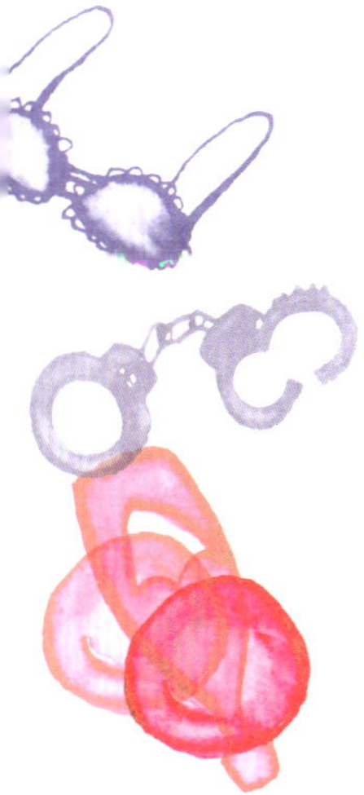

The Divorce Registry II

- *Selection of black lace quarter-cup bras & knickers from La Perla – 34 B,*
- *Silk negliges from Sabbia Rosa – black, cream, turquoise – size 38*
- *Swarovski crystal-encrusted whip*
- *Many cases of Krug*
- *Chelsea Club membership*
- *Course of Botox and laser treatments at The Harley Clinic*
- *Pebble by Mari-Ruth Oda*
- *Handyman*

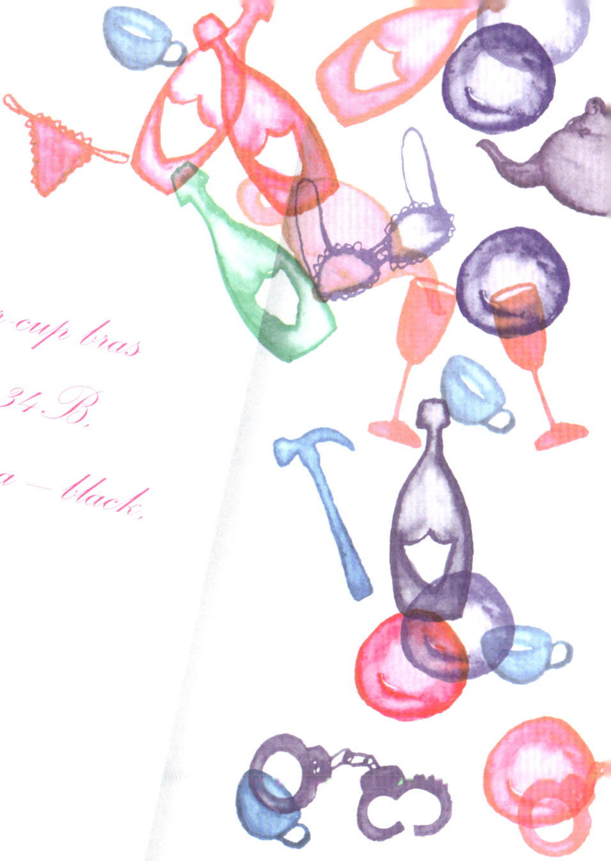

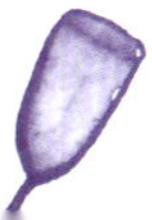

It is important that you don't become a sponge. In the same way that you only really have to buy a pressie if you go to the wedding, you can't expect pressies without throwing a divorce party.

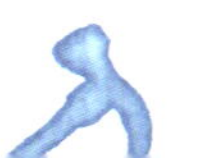

The Divorce Party

The Divorce Party need not be extravagant or lavish but it should be a celebration of you and your freedom (regardless of who left whom). As such it should be shamelessly self-indulgent.

Music to get divorced by:

1. Love Stinks — J. Geils Band
2. Goodbye To You — Scandal
3. I Will Survive — Gloria Gaynor
4. Go Your Own Way — Fleetwood Mac
5. 50 Ways To Leave Your Lover — Paul Simon
6. Hit The Road Jack — Ray Charles
7. You're So Vain — Carly Simon
8. The Thrill Is Gone — B.B. King
9. Time For Me To Fly — REO Speedwagon
10. Release Me — Engelbert Humperdinck
11. Sail On — Commodores
12. Harden My Heart — Quarterflash
13. I Hate Myself For Loving You — Joan Jett and The Blackhearts
14. Whatever Will Be, Will Be (Que Sera, Sera) — Doris Day
15. Here's A Quarter (Call Someone Who Cares) — Travis Tritt
16. Jive Talkin' — The Bee Gees
17. Let's Call The Whole Thing Off — Harry Connick, Jr.
18. Lonesome Loser — Little River Band
19. Separate Ways (Worlds Apart) — Journey
20. Sisters Are Doin' It For Themselves — Aretha Franklin

CHANEL
NO.5

Divorce party entertainment:

Your wedding video played in rewind – the bit where you take off your ring, walk back down the aisle and drive off...

The one thing you must absolutely show off with pride at your Divorce Party is your UNENGAGEMENT RING. Your Unengagement Ring should be everything you wanted your engagement ring to be but wasn't. It should be worn on your middle finger.

Getting Even

There will be the temptation at almost every stage of your divorce, and after, to get even. After all, "Hell hath no fury…" even if you weren't technically scorned. Getting even can range from the merely puerile practical jokes to the most sinister of calculated MI5 plans to terminate with extreme prejudice.

As a friend said to me, "If your ex-husband didn't completely annoy the shit out of you, then he wouldn't be your ex-husband, would he?" He had a valid point.

If you are vacating the marital home, you could just do inanely annoying things which will cause irritation but no long-term inconvenience such as unscrewing every single light bulb and disconnecting the gas/electricity/water supply. For more sustained damage, there's always the age-old trick of leaving fresh prawns in the curtain rails to rot and fill the house with a fetid stench.

A friend in Tokyo told me how, for months after his wife left, he found the crotch cut out of random pairs of underpants and trousers. They had all been left carefully in their right place so no damage could be detected until they were needed.

If you don't think you have received an adequate portion of the marital assets and wish to hurt him financially, you could dial the speaking clock in Argentina and leave the phone off the hook. A very angry girlfriend reported all her ex-husband's credit cards stolen while he was travelling on a business trip. He was left stranded in Kazakhstan for three days.

Nothing causes stress like travel. You could call the anonymous terrorist hotline, naming your ex-husband as a suspect therefore ensuring all manner of obstacles whenever he goes within a ten-mile radius of an airport.

There are any number of ways to embarrass him at work. I heard of a woman who was in the middle of divorcing her adulterous husband turning up at his office with all his dirty laundry. She tipped the entire bag onto his secretary's desk in full view of all his colleagues saying. *"You're fucking him   you can do his fucking laundry!"*

Anonymously informing the relevant industry watchdog could be fun. Imagine. his professional reputation forever suspect!

Everyone fears and loathes the tax man. They're like the Stasi – always urging people to inform on their neighbours. friends and families. Here's an honest mistake to make: you thought you were doing HMS Revenue & Customs a service. calling to let them know about your ex-husband's Jersey bank account. (Obviously. you do this only AFTER you have received your settlement in full.)

Really. the inconvenience. pain and destruction you could cause is limited only by your imagination and sense of potential remorse at doing any of this.

THE WHIFF OF FRAUD AND SCANDAL CAN NEVER BE QUITE EXTINGUISHED.

Rising Above It

If you are tempted to exact revenge in any of the above ways, I apologise now for putting the ideas into your head. I don't recommend it.

Living well is indeed the best revenge, so concentrate all your energies into living as well as you can and a great deal more so than you would ever have done if you had stayed married. To do this, you must rise above the emotional swamp and navigate your own lovely path around it. The greatest advice I ever received is to strive for total indifference towards your ex-husband – indifference to what he says, what he does, whom he sees and where he is.

If you have children, you will necessarily have to have more contact with your ex-husband than you would probably wish. It is a good idea to keep this to the written word. There can be no misinterpretation if your wording is clear, no accusations of who did or didn't say what, and no instant emotional reaction that you cannot check.

There are some simple tools that make clear, unemotional, detached communication easier. The main thing to bear in mind is "What do I need to get out of this particular exchange?" Keep everything you write focused and relevant to that one thing you need, and don't allow this need to be an emotional one. In responding to an email with any derogatory or inflammatory remarks, hit reply, delete all unnecessary information and distil it to purely what you have to deal with. Sounds obvious but it wasn't to me until someone pointed out its benefit. Do not get dragged into defending yourself or descending to insult. It is simply a waste of energy.

I will infuriatingly point out here that your ex-husband was a man you once loved and chose to spend the rest of your life with. He may have changed but you did think he was a gem of some sort or other once upon a time. If he didn't know how to push your buttons then you were probably not really ever married at all.

Do honour to yourself, to the memory and to one of the biggest decisions you ever made. Behave with dignity. It isn't easy, but it really is the best thing to do.

> "When two people decide to get a divorce, it isn't a sign that they 'don't understand' one another, but a sign that they have, at last, begun to."

Helen Rowland,
English-American writer 1876-1950

Looking After Me

Lots of people you know have done it and lots of people you know are probably doing it, but that doesn't make the whole business of divorce any easier. When finally you come through the courts and the endless rounds of negotiation, the drama and trauma, the anger and pain, the relief or jubilation or whatever it is you feel can be short-lived. This is when you have to look after yourself. I don't mean having candlelit aromatherapy oil baths and eating granola. I mean really looking after the whole you, inside and out.

As relieved as you might be at not having to live with the intolerable sod ever again, there are a great number of things you have to learn to do again on your own. Seek advice, ask for help – whether it be from a therapist, a guru, the plumber, your mother or best friend. Just for a little while, ask for your own needs to be met and fulfilled. Surround yourself with good people, real friends and strong supporters, people who make you laugh and feel good about yourself, people who respect the decision you made, people who do not judge.

Looking after yourself also means looking after your body and your appearance – your face, your skin, your hands, your feet, your hair, and your bikini line… Do NOT fall into disarray or everyone will say your ex is better off without you, and you may start to feel that way yourself. It seems shallow but it isn't. It's called self-respect.

Have fun. Have a lot of it.
BE NAUGHTY.

Giggle. *Laugh.* Love yourself.

Whatever you think you did wrong, it really wasn't so bad.

Meeting Your Ex-husba

Hopefully, your social lives will have parted naturally somewhere down the middle. He will have retained some of your friends and you his. If so, there will be the odd social occasion where you will coincide, and wise hosts will usually have the grace and foresight to have alerted both of you. It is on these occasions that you will likely meet the new woman in your ex-husband's life. She can range from being a squeaky bendy thing to a woman of surprising form and substance. Surprising because you didn't think any woman of form and substance could possibly find your ex-husband remotely attractive – physically, intellectually or emotionally. Just remember, you once did.

How you feel about her is something you keep very private and if you need to share, do so to a very select group. If she is a mere toy of limited mental capacity, be nice, be sweet, be gracious to her. Her squeaky bendiness will speak for itself, in your favour. Your poor ex-husband probably deserves some simple pleasure.

If you are met with a "spitting image" of yourself, however, it can be very unnerving. Gather yourself, like you would gather a horse to go through his paces, take a deep breath, think of something funny and flash your most dazzling smile. The sort of smile that says, "I really don't care and I

genuinely hope you are happy with each other." No point in being a dog in the manger about things – she will discover all his fallibilities soon enough, and perhaps they won't bother her as they did you.

Bear in mind that you will likely be someone else's ex-husband's new girlfriend at some stage. Think how you would want to be treated by his ex-wife.

A good friend of mine lives by the motto, "Kill them with kindness." I have finally learned the true power of this, although I am not always able to apply it. I'm not suggesting you want

nd's New Girlfriend

to actually befriend your ex-husband's new girlfriend, and she will be as reluctant as you to do lunch, but to be met with kindness, openness and old fashioned good manners when you were expecting cold hostility is very unsettling and rather takes the wind out of one's sails. It will also infuriate your ex when his girlfriend says anything at all positive about you, as he will no doubt have painted a deeply biased picture of the impossible harridan that he perceives you to have been to him.

It goes without saying that anyone your ex-husband dates or subsequently marries is in every way inferior to you.

Future husbands and everything in between

I don't think divorce makes you a man-hater. If anything, a good number of divorcées start wondering relatively quickly where and how they are going to meet, if not their next husband, then at least a man worth a dalliance.

It's all well and good believing in that trite chain-email philosophy, "Work as if you dont need money, dance as if no one is watching and love as if you've never been hurt," but the fact of the matter is you have been hurt – and therefore you can't just exit a divorce and throw yourself at high speed with wild abandon into the intoxicating, tempestuous, emotionally wrought and fraught whirlwind of love.

Where indeed does one meet Mr. Right-for-a-drink, Mr. Right-for-dinner, Mr. Right-for-a-bedroom-workout or just Mr. Right Now?

Friends will tell you to get "OUT THERE" but WHERE THE HELL IS "THERE"? Where do the fun, loving, caring, considerate, intelligent, available men abound ?

"THERE," I found, is a head space, a mental state of truly feeling awesome and attractive and when you feel awesome and attractive, you feel safe enough to be a little open – not laid bare but just a little open – and things begin to happen.

YOUNGER MEN are worshipful, have energy and virility and accept without question the authority of an older woman. They are playful and sweet, sometimes wilful and petulant, and they are fun. I would probably get a Labrador puppy instead – dogs understand when you tell them their friends can't come inside.

PLAYBOYS know how to charm, to wine, to dine, to send flowers and good lingerie, but the relationship can be much like the lingerie – exquisitely crafted, expensive, feels good on your skin but is limited in its uses.

DIVORCING MEN – honestly do you want to hang out with someone who is going through what your ex-husband just went through? That much déjà-vu can't be good for anyone. What's more, you'll want to dispense advice and we know how much men hate listening to advice.

MARRIED MEN should just be avoided. Yes, they sometimes leave their wives but this is the exception, not the rule. Do you have the desire or fortitude to be available to someone who is not very available to you?

Divine Divorcees Wall

Jerry Hall
Divorced after 9
years of marriage.

Joanna Lumley
Divorced abruptly after
4 months of marriage.

Audrey Hepburn
Divorced twice. her first marriage lasted 14
years and her second 13 years.

Ivana Trump
Divorced 3 times.
The shortest
marriage lasted 2
years and the longest
15 years.

Katharine Hepburn
Divorced after 6 years
of marriage.

Elizabeth Taylor
Divorced 7 times.
The shortest marriage lasted
8 months. the longest
10 years.

Diana Mitford
Divorced once after 2
years of marriage.

Amy Johnson
Divorced after 6 years
of marriage.

# of Fame

Rita Hayworth
Divorced 5 times.
The shortest marriage
lasted 2 years, the
longest 6 years.

Lana Turner
Divorced 7 times.

Angelina Jolie
Divorced twice,
both marriages lasted
3 years.

Estée Lauder
Divorced after 9 years of
marriage but remarried her
ex-husband 3 years later.

Vivien Leigh
Divorced twice, her first marriage lasted 8 years,
her second 20 years.

Demi Moore
Divorced twice,
her first marriage lasted
5 years and her
second 13 years.

Princess Diana
Divorced after 15 years of marriage.

Zsa Zsa Gabor
Divorced 8 times,
The longest marriage
lasted 13 years.

"Divorce.
A resumption of
diplomatic relations
and rectification
of boundaries."

Ambrose Bierce

They say life is about *cycles*, that everything comes full circle. So in the beginning you met, you were courteous, you had boundaries. Then you fell in love, got married, removed those boundaries, became familiar. Familiarity bred contempt. In your contempt you started to despise each other, you argued, you fought, you grew apart, so you separated. In separating you fought some more and finally you divorced. And so, you are back to the beginning…

About the author
AMY ALLEN
Amy, formerly Allen, now once again Poon is the best-selling author of *This Little Piggy went to Prada*. She is a mother of a six-year-old and recently divorced. Amy graduated from Oxford with a degree in Japanese and has lived in Geneva, Tokyo, Sydney and Singapore before settling back in London, in the deepest darkest depths of Nappy Valley on a budget settlement. Her immense relief at and new-found joy in no longer being married inspired the creation of "This Little Piggy got Divorced".
www.thislittlepiggywenttoprada.com

About the illustrator
ZEBBY EUNKYUNG KANG
Korean born, UK based Zebby joined the Piggy Team while studying fashion at the London College of Fashion. Since her Piggy debut, Zebby has worked for clients all over the world, including Vogue, Numero, Boutique1, Jaeger, Matches and Penguin Books. She currently lives and studies in Brighton and works at Laines Organic Farm in Cuckfield, Sussex.
www.zebby.net

About the designer
MARTIN MC LOUGHLIN
Martin McLoughlin founded Studio McLoughlin in 1998 and has won many design awards both in the UK and the US. He fathered Piggy on a blind date.
www.studiomcloughlin.co.uk

Just Divorced

merci

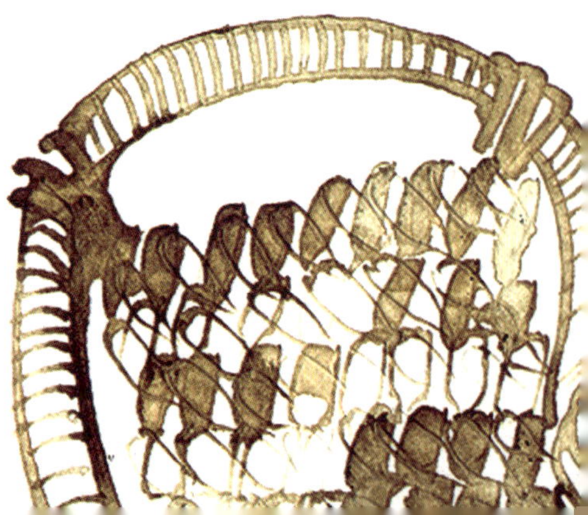

CAFE DE fleur
CAFE DE fleur
LE FIGARO
Duel au sommet

“For some reason, we see divorce as a
signal of failure, despite the fact that each of us
has a right, and an obligation, to rectify any
other mistake we make in life.”

Joyce Brothers